Blue C
Comeback

Lesley Ward

✳ Smithsonian

Contributing Author

Allison Duarte, M.A

Consultants

Tamieka Grizzle, Ed.D.
K–5 STEM Lab Instructor
Harmony Leland Elementary School

Alison Cawood
Citizen Science Coordinator,
Smithsonian

Publishing Credits

Rachelle Cracchiolo, M.S.Ed., *Publisher*
Conni Medina, M.A.Ed., *Managing Editor*
Diana Kenney, M.A.Ed., NBCT, *Content Director*
Véronique Bos, *Creative Director*
June Kikuchi, *Content Director*
Robin Erickson, *Art Director*
Seth Rogers, *Editor*
Mindy Duits, *Senior Graphic Designer*
Smithsonian Science Education Center

Image Credits: p.5 Corbis/Getty Images; p.7 Science Source/Getty Images; p.8, p.14, p.16 (both), p.17, p.18, p.23 © Smithsonian; pp.20–21 M. Timothy O'Keefe/Alamy; all other images from iStock and/or Shutterstock.

Library of Congress Cataloging-in-Publication Data

Names: Ward, Lesley, author.
Title: Blue crab comeback / Lesley Ward.
Description: Huntington Beach, CA : Teacher Created Materials, [2018] | Audience: K to grade 3. | Includes index.
Identifiers: LCCN 2017060494 (print) | LCCN 2017061413 (ebook) | ISBN 9781493869305 (e-book) | ISBN 9781493866908 (pbk.)
Subjects: LCSH: Blue crab--Conservation--Chesapeake Bay (Md. and Va.)--Juvenile literature. | Blue crab--Chesapeake Bay (Md. and Va.)--Juvenile literature. | Blue crab fisheries--Juvenile literature. | Crabs--Conservation--Chesapeake Bay (Md. and Va.)--Juvenile literature. | Crabs--Juvenile literature. | Chesapeake Bay (Md. and Va.)--Ecology--Juvenile literature.
Classification: LCC QL444.M33 (ebook) | LCC QL444.M33 W3575 2018 (print) | DDC 595.3/86--dc23
LC record available at https://lccn.loc.gov/2017060494

Smithsonian

Teacher Created Materials

5301 Oceanus Drive
Huntington Beach, CA 92649-1030
www.tcmpub.com

ISBN 978-1-4938-6690-8

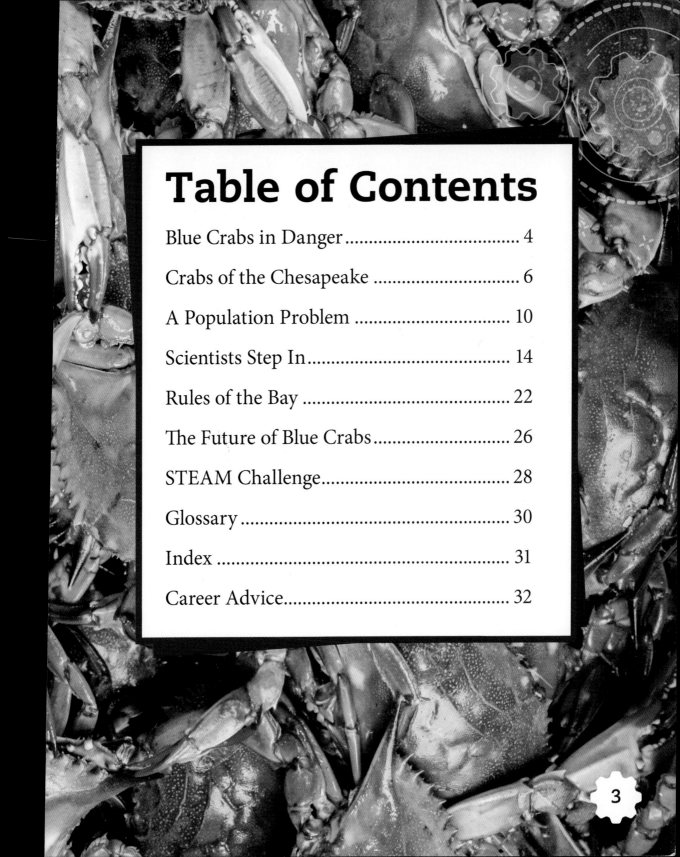

Table of Contents

Blue Crabs in Danger 4

Crabs of the Chesapeake 6

A Population Problem 10

Scientists Step In...................................... 14

Rules of the Bay 22

The Future of Blue Crabs........................... 26

STEAM Challenge...................................... 28

Glossary 30

Index 31

Career Advice.. 32

Blue Crabs in Danger

Millions of blue crabs are caught in the Chesapeake Bay each year. People love to eat blue crab meat because it is sweet. Crabs are served in restaurants around the world. But there is a big problem brewing in the bay. Blue crabs are in trouble. Their population is shrinking. Why? The two main reasons are overfishing and changes in their habitat. This affects watermen who work long hours to catch blue crabs to make money. Soon, there could be no more crabs left to catch! If this happens, thousands of people will lose their jobs.

Scientists and watermen have teamed up to prevent this disaster. Scientists catch the crabs and release them back into the bay. They study the lives of blue crabs. Watermen collect data about the crabs while they work on their boats. Scientists and watermen are working together to save blue crabs.

This man catches blue crabs in the Chesapeake Bay.

Crabs of the Chesapeake

Blue crabs get their name from their sapphire-blue claws. Males' claws are all blue. Females have red highlights on the tips of their **pincers** (PIN-suhrz). All blue crabs have brown or olive-green shells that measure up to 23 centimeters (9 inches) across. A blue crab's shell is called a *carapace* (KEHR-uh-puhs).

Blue crabs have four pairs of legs. Three pairs are for walking. The rear two legs are shaped like paddles. They are used for swimming. Blue crabs are close relatives of shrimp and lobster. They are *invertebrates*, which means they have no spines.

One of the largest populations of blue crabs is in the Chesapeake Bay. The bay is located in the United States and is bordered by Maryland and Virginia.

Chesapeake Bay

A blue crab molts.

Shell Shedders

As a crab grows, it sheds its shell and grows a bigger one. This process is called *molting*. The hypodermis (high-poh-DUHR-miss), a layer of cells under the shell, produces **enzymes**. These enzymes loosen the tissues connecting the old shell to the crab. A soft shell grows underneath. The crab absorbs water, causing it to swell. The old shell breaks, and the crab wiggles out. The new shell is soft, but hardens in a few days.

Blue crabs move around a lot during their lives. When they are **larva**, they live in salty water far down in the bay. As they grow, they swim toward land. Young crabs hide from **predators** in marshes and sea grass close to shore.

Blue crabs usually live three to four years. They become adults in 12 to 18 months. This is the age when they can begin to produce young. In warm weather, blue crabs live in shallow water. In winter, they hibernate in deep water. Female blue crabs **mate** only once in their lives. But they spawn, or lay eggs, multiple times.

Female crabs take a dangerous journey to lay their eggs. They swim to the mouth of the Chesapeake Bay to spawn in the salty water of the ocean. They are in danger of being eaten by predators on the trip. Watermen might also catch female crabs in nets. The females that make it to the spawning ground can lay more than three million eggs!

female crab with eggs

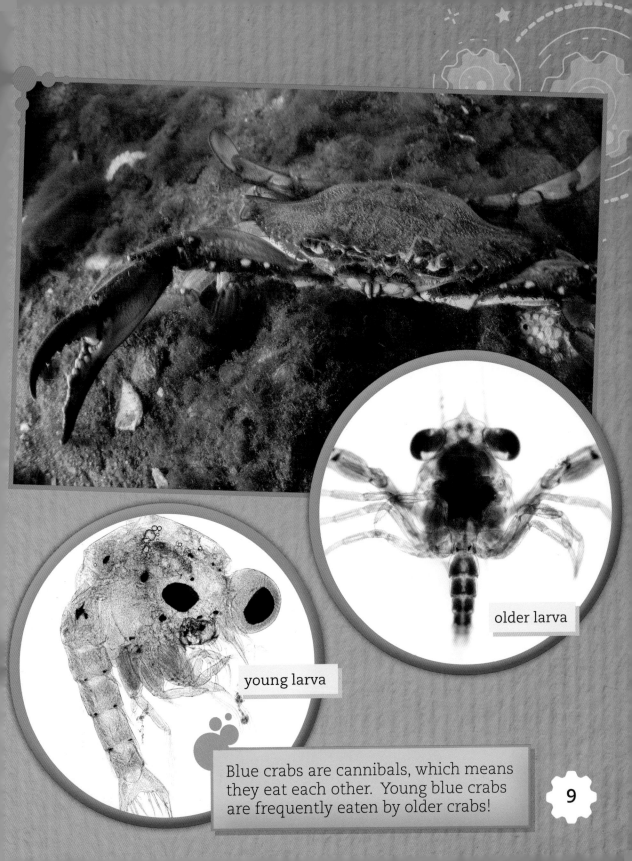

older larva

young larva

Blue crabs are cannibals, which means
they eat each other. Young blue crabs
are frequently eaten by older crabs!

A Population Problem

The number of blue crabs in the Chesapeake Bay was very low in 2008. This was a huge problem. The crab shortage hurt people who lived and worked on the bay. Watermen depended on blue crabs for their jobs. Restaurants needed crabs to feed customers.

Scientists worried about blue crabs, too. They feared that a shortage of blue crabs might lead to problems with other species. Blue crabs play a big role in the **food chain** of the bay.

Many animals in the bay depend on blue crabs for food. Birds, small mammals, and fish eat blue crabs. These animals are eaten by larger animals.

If the crabs died out, larger animals could follow. This would have a big impact on the bay's **ecosystem**.

A greater yellowlegs feasts on a tiny crab.

A great blue heron catches a blue crab.

When you eat a soft-shell crab, you eat the entire animal! This includes its head, claws, legs, and carapace.

11

Human Impact

Watermen have tough jobs. They arrive at the dock very early in the morning. They begin the day by checking the gear on their boats. They repair their traps, called crab pots, so that big crabs cannot escape. They cut chunks of eel to use as **bait**, and they head out to the bay to look for the floats attached to their pots.

A waterman can pull up as many as five hundred pots per day. Some pull up the heavy pots by hand. Others have motors that pull them up. They are excited when pots are full of crabs. In 2008, the pots were empty most days. This was a disaster!

The watermen of the Chesapeake Bay need a large crab population to earn a living. There is a high demand for blue crabs. Crabs are sold to seafood companies and restaurants. But, if there are no crabs, there is no money to be made.

crab boat

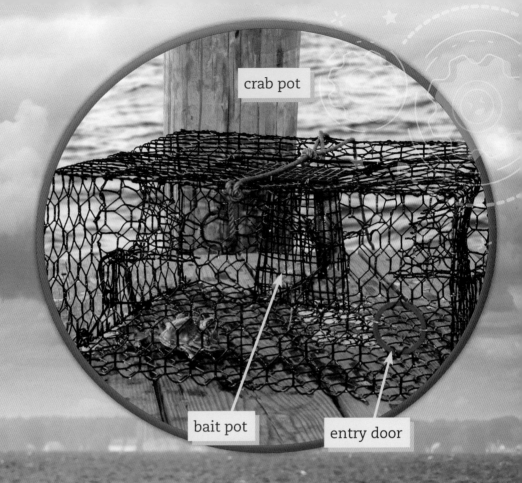

crab pot

bait pot

entry door

How a Crab Pot Works

In the past, watermen used handheld nets and baskets to catch crabs. This was difficult and took lots of time. Today, they use traps made of wire mesh that they can leave in the water for several days. The traps have doors that allow crabs to go inside to eat bait, but they cannot get out.

Scientists Step In

Local officials worried about the empty crab pots. Thousands of watermen and seafood businesses depended on blue crabs for money. Many people lost their jobs in 2008 because of the crab shortage. There was no time to waste! The region was **declared** a disaster area. The U.S. government gave money to help.

Officials wanted to know what was happening to the crabs. They asked scientists for help. The scientists knew a lot about crabs and the ecosystem of the bay. But they needed to collect data to learn why the population was so low.

They planned to trap blue crabs in the bay. Then, they could study them and collect all the data they could. Were the crabs' diets changing? Were they moving to new parts of the bay? Were female crabs laying enough eggs? They had to find out why the number of crabs was shrinking. Then, they could try to fix the problem.

Marine biologists are scientists who study plants and animals that live in salt water. The ocean is their lab!

Scientists began to monitor blue crabs. They caught and released crabs 30 times in one year. It was important for scientists to take the same steps every time. This helped make sure that the data was accurate.

They set up four stations to catch crabs. The first one was at the head of the Rhode River. The head of a river is where the river begins. Two more stations were set up at the river's mouth. The mouth of a river is where the river flows into a large body of water. This river flows into the Chesapeake Bay. The fourth station was out in the bay.

Scientists used a netted trap called an otter trawl to catch crabs. The trawl was pulled along the bottom of the water by a boat. The trawl was always in the water for exactly 10 minutes.

The trawl was then pulled back on the boat. Scientists emptied the nets into big buckets. Fish that had been caught were thrown back into the bay. Then, the scientists studied the blue crabs.

This tagged blue crab was found in a river near the Chesapeake.

Marine biologists pull a trawl out of the Rhode River.

Trawling for Blue Crabs

A trawl is made of several parts. It has two heavy doors, which weigh the trawl down. Each trawl also has a row of floats at the top of the net. Floats are light objects, which help keep the net open. Each trawl has a chain attached to it. As a boat pulls a trawl through the sand, the chain scares the crabs and they jump into the net.

Marine biologists collected data about each crab. They measured each crab's shell. They wrote whether it was male or female and estimated its age. The health of every crab was observed and noted. Did the crab look healthy? Or did it look sick? Was it missing any limbs? Finally, they noted whether the crab was molting. If so, they determined the stage of molting.

After data was collected, most crabs were thrown back into the water. But a few were kept for tagging. The scientists attached a search tag with a wire to each crab's shell. The tag had an ID and phone number on it. Then, these crabs were released back into the bay, too.

Watermen who caught tagged crabs called the phone number and reported where and when they caught them. This data helped scientists track the movements of the blue crabs.

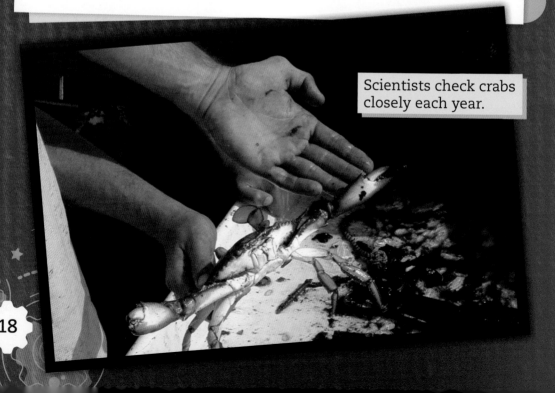

Scientists check crabs closely each year.

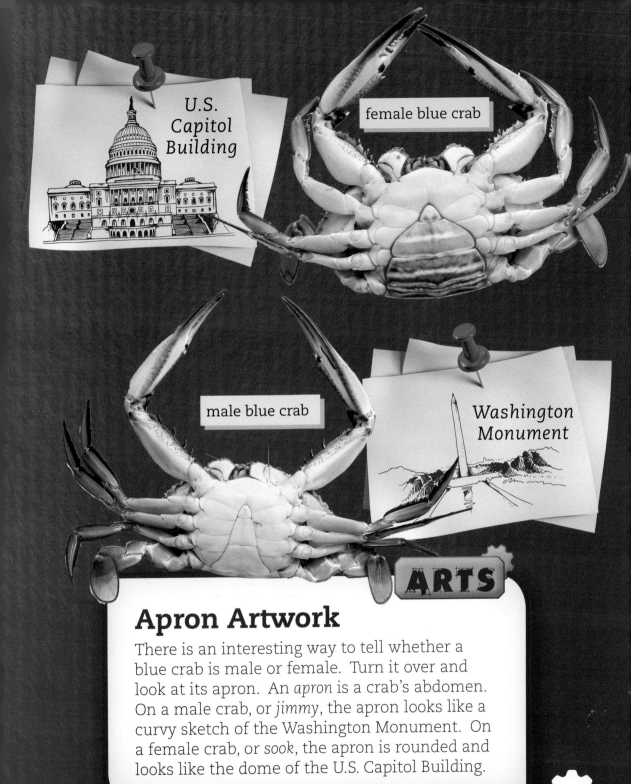

U.S. Capitol Building

female blue crab

male blue crab

Washington Monument

ARTS

Apron Artwork

There is an interesting way to tell whether a blue crab is male or female. Turn it over and look at its apron. An *apron* is a crab's abdomen. On a male crab, or *jimmy*, the apron looks like a curvy sketch of the Washington Monument. On a female crab, or *sook*, the apron is rounded and looks like the dome of the U.S. Capitol Building.

The Results

Scientists looked at the data they collected. They figured out why the crabs were disappearing. There were many reasons. The biggest one was overfishing. Watermen caught too many crabs each year. This was especially true for females. Thousands of female crabs were trapped as they went to lay eggs in the mouth of the bay. Some females traveled more than 240 kilometers (150 miles) to spawn. This put them at great risk.

Predators in the water were another problem. Predators, such as red drum fish, ate a lot of young crabs. Water pollution also hurt the crabs. Dirty water in the bay caused large algae blooms. The algae blocked the sun. The lack of light killed underwater grass. Crabs need grass to hide from predators. The algae also killed the worms and clams that these crabs eat.

red drum fish

Sea turtles are predators of blue crabs.

If a blue crab loses a limb or a claw, it can grow it back. This is part of the molting process. It is called *regeneration*.

Rules of the Bay

The Chesapeake Bay is large. It is bordered by two states. This made it a challenge to protect the blue crabs. People in Maryland and Virginia had to work together. Leaders worked to figure out how to stop overfishing. Watermen and scientists joined them. They asked the managers of fisheries, places that sell fish, to help.

The officials listened to everyone. Then, they made strict rules to help save blue crabs. Many of the rules are still in place.

The rules shortened the crabbing season. They limited the number of days a week that watermen could trap crabs. There were special rules for female crabs. One rule reduced the number of females that could be trapped. Watermen could no longer catch females that were on their way to spawn.

Dredging in winter was also banned. Dredging is a process that scoops crabs out of the mud as they hibernate. Watermen who broke these rules had to pay a fine.

Watermen use a special tool to measure blue crabs.

Anson Hines, of the Smithsonian Environmental Research Center, holds a blue crab with a tracker attached to its shell.

Counting Blue Crabs

The Blue Crab Winter Dredge Survey collects data about the population of blue crabs in the Chesapeake Bay each year. Fifteen sites are dredged. Scientists count the crabs that are trapped at each site. The average number of crabs caught in an area is called the *density*. This number helps estimate the total number of crabs. Then, officials can figure out how many crabs can be trapped each season.

Many watermen did not like the new rules. How would they make money? But they knew the rules were necessary. There would be no jobs if there were no blue crabs. The overfishing had to stop. But full nets were not the only danger to crabs. Other measures had to be taken.

Officials set limits on how much pollution could flow into the bay. This reduced the algae blooms that killed underwater grass. Boaters had to slow down in shallow water so their wakes, or waves, didn't damage the grass.

The measures worked. There were 292 million blue crabs in the bay in 2008. Then, the rules were put in place. The number of crabs jumped to 396 million the next year. In 2010, there were 663 million crabs. Watermen and scientists were happy. But they couldn't relax. They knew the number of crabs would continue to go up and down in the future.

Manhole covers remind people to keep pollution out of the bay.

During the 2015 crabbing season, 22.6 million kilograms (50 million pounds) of blue crabs were caught in and around the Chesapeake Bay.

The Future of Blue Crabs

The future of blue crabs in the Chesapeake Bay is uncertain. One year, the crab pots might be full. The next year, they might be empty. The number of blue crabs is affected by overfishing and changes in habitat. There is still a lot of work to do.

Scientists continue to study the lives of blue crabs. They trap and release them to gather data. They share what they find with officials who then decide how many blue crabs can be caught each season. They make new rules to help protect crabs.

Scientists and watermen must continue to work as a team. Their goal is to keep a healthy blue crab population. If they do, watermen will earn money. People will be able to order blue crabs in restaurants. Most importantly, blue crabs will continue to thrive for years to come.

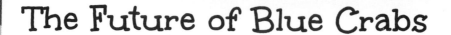

crab cakes

boiled blue crabs

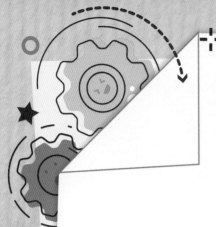

STEAM CHALLENGE

Define the Problem

Engineers often make small models of large systems. They use the models to test ideas. They see how the systems work. You have been asked to help solve the problem of pollution in the Chesapeake Bay. Your task is to make a model of a water filtration system. Engineers may use your design to make a large-scale system in the bay.

Constraints: You may only use one man-made item. All other materials must be found in nature.

Criteria: You will pour muddy water with mulch through the system. The system should collect clear water without other matter.

Research and Brainstorm

How does pollution harm crabs? How are scientists working to fix the problem? What is the purpose of a filter?

Design and Build

Sketch your design. What purpose will each part serve? What materials will work best? Build the model.

Test and Improve

Pour muddy water through the system. Observe the water that is collected. Did the filter work? How can you improve it? Modify your design, and try again.

Reflect and Share

Could you use different materials? Could you test the model a new way? Could this system serve another purpose? How does water pollution affect humans?

Glossary

accurate—free from errors or mistakes

algae—simple plants and plant-like organisms that usually grow in water

bait—something that is used to attract animals or fish so that they can be caught

declared—said something in a public or official way

dredging—removing mud from the bottom of a body of water

ecosystem—community of living and nonliving things in a particular environment

enzymes—chemical substances that help cause reactions (as in the digestion of food)

food chain—a chain of events in which one type of living thing is food for another type of living thing

habitat—the natural home of an animal, plant, or other organism

larva—the young form of an animal

mate—to come or bring together to produce young

pincers—the front claws of a crab

population—a group of individuals of the same species that live in the same place at the same time

predators—animals that live by killing and eating other animals

wakes—waves left by boats as they move through water

watermen—people who earn their living harvesting fish, shrimp, oysters, or crabs

Index

algae blooms, 20, 24

apron, 19

Blue Crab Winter Dredge Survey, 23

Chesapeake Bay, 4–6, 8, 10, 12, 16, 22–23, 25–26, 28

crab pot, 12–14, 26

density, 23

eel, 12

hypodermis, 7

jimmy, 19

marine biologists, 15, 17–18

Maryland, 6, 22

red drum fish, 20

Rhode River, 16–17

sook, 19

trawl, 16–17

U.S. Capitol Building, 19

Virginia, 6, 22

Washington Monument, 19

Do you want to help aquatic animals?
Here are some tips to get you started.

"Many problems require huge amounts of data to create solutions. We need to work with people who are experts in different fields to find the best information about each topic. That way, we can all combine the best information to solve problems." —Katy Newcomer, Research Technician, Smithsonian Environmental Research Center

"Scientific data can be very useful for solving problems. However, data by itself isn't enough. Fixing big problems requires scientists and communities to work together. They have to use data to find solutions that work for everyone. Being a good communicator and a good team player are just as important as collecting good data." —Alison Cawood, Ph.D., Citizen Science Coordinator, Smithsonian Environmental Research Center